THE WORLD OF ANIME AND MANGA

THE WORLD OF ANIME

by Carla Mooney

BrightPoint Press

San Diego, CA

BrightPoint Press

an imprint of ReferencePoint Press, Inc.
Printed in the United States
For more information, contact:

BrightPoint Press
PO Box 27779
San Diego, CA 92198
www.BrightPointPress.com

LIBRARY OF CONGRESS CATALOGING-IN-PUBLICATION DATA

Names: Mooney, Carla, author.
Title: The World of Anime / by Carla Mooney.
Description: San Diego, CA: ReferencePoint Press, Inc., 2024 | Series: The World of Anime and Manga | Audience: Grade 7 to 9 | Includes bibliographical references and index.
Identifiers: ISBN 9781678207564 (hardcover) | ISBN 9781678207571 (eBook)
The complete Library of Congress record is available at www.loc.gov.

CONTENTS

AT A GLANCE

- Anime is a type of animation developed in Japan in the early 1900s.
- Anime is known for its colorful artwork, energetic characters, and exciting stories.
- There are many genres of anime, including shonen, shojo, and seinen.
- Anime animators give characters large eyes to show emotion.
- The first feature-length anime was released in 1958. It was called *Hakujaden*.
- *Dragon Ball* is one of the most popular anime of all time. It was released in 1986.
- In 2003, the anime movie *Spirited Away* won the Academy Award for Best Animated Feature.
- For many years, artists drew anime by hand. Today, most anime is created with computers.

- Many anime are adapted into different languages for fans outside Japan.
- Anime has become a huge industry that earns billions of dollars each year.
- Some anime fans dress up as their favorite characters. This activity is called cosplay.
- Popular anime stories and characters have expanded into video games and other merchandise.

INTRODUCTION

DISCOVERING ANIME

The doorbell rings, and Lucas runs to open the door. His best friend, Riley, stands on the porch. She has a big grin on her face and a plate of cookies in her hands. "My mom sent these over," she says. "We can eat them while we watch the show."

In the kitchen, the two friends huddle around Riley's laptop. She pulls up a streaming episode of *Attack on Titan*. For Lucas, watching anime is a new experience. He is used to traditional American television shows and cartoons. Japanese anime is different. Anime has a distinctive look and sound. Riley had explained to Lucas that there are several categories

***Attack on Titan** began as a popular manga series before being adapted into an anime.*

Watching anime has become a popular pastime among young people all over the world.

of anime. Each has a target audience and common features.

Lucas is quickly drawn into the show's fictional world. In this first episode, it seems like an ordinary day for ten-year-old Eren and his friend Mikasa. But the calm does not last long. Lucas stares at the screen as enormous creatures called Titans climb over the city walls. The Titans attack people around them. They destroy buildings. Eren and Mikasa run for their lives. Lucas feels his heart race with the action on-screen. The Titans overtake the city. Eren sees his mother being eaten by one of the monsters. Lucas quietly wipes a tear from his eye. Eren promises to avenge the deaths of his mother and others. As the credits roll, Lucas turns to Riley. He says, "Let's watch another episode!"

A DISTINCTIVE STYLE OF ANIMATION

Anime is a style of **animation**. It was first developed in Japan in the early 1900s. Over the years, anime has grown into a popular form of entertainment around the world.

Millions of fans worldwide watch anime television series and films. Communities of anime fans attend conventions and buy **merchandise**. Some fans create art and dress up as their favorite characters.

Many people learn about anime from a family member or friend. Asa Suehira is the chief content officer of Crunchyroll, an anime streaming service. He says, "The love of anime is now being passed from generation to generation, and if you go to any anime convention, you will see parents and children alike enjoying it. It's something special to see parents passing the torch."[1] According to Suehira, anime has become much more than a style of animation. For many people, anime has become an important part of life.

Many anime fans enjoy collecting action figures of characters, such as Boku from My Hero Academia.

1

WHAT IS ANIME?

Anime began in Japan. This animation style is known for its colorful visuals, energetic characters, and exciting stories. Since its creation, anime has spread worldwide. Today, people watch anime movies and television shows in many countries. Anime is translated into many languages and enjoyed by fans across the globe.

COMMON CHARACTERISTICS

There are many types of anime. Most people recognize anime by the way it looks. Many anime shows use a similar art style. For example, characters often have large, expressive eyes. The eyes often take up

Some anime fans believe hair color is linked to a character's personality traits. For example, many fans think blue represents shyness.

much of a character's face. Animators use a character's eyes to show emotions. Also, characters often have large heads and wild, brightly colored hair.

Animators **exaggerate** a character's expressions and actions to illustrate emotions. For example, large tears show a character is embarrassed or upset. Expressions and movements reveal a character's personality.

Anime series use several common camera effects. The camera often **pans** across a scene. It may zoom in for a dramatic close-up. Angled shots are also used in many anime series. Anime also features brilliant colors and vivid lighting. This style is eye-catching for viewers.

Anime is also known for its complex characters and storylines. Characters have

ANIME STUDIOS AROUND JAPAN

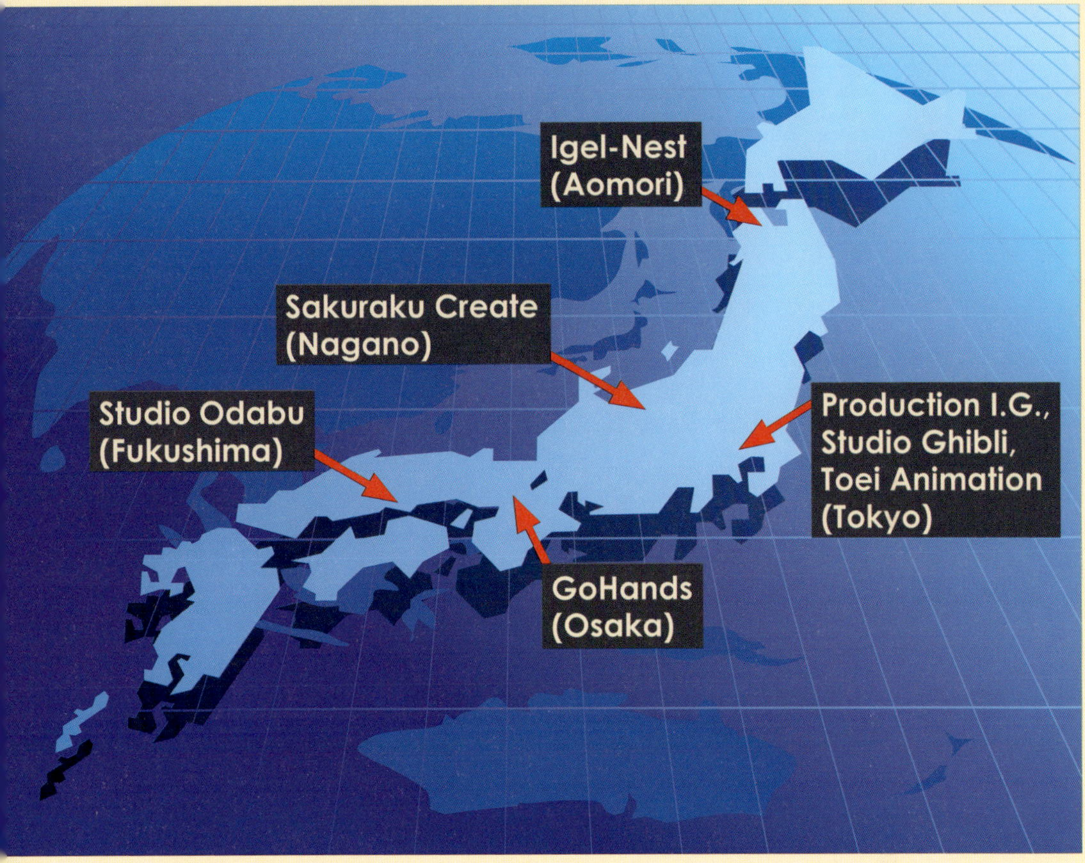

Anime studios are found throughout Japan. But many of them are based in Tokyo.

many personality traits. These features make them more realistic. Storylines take place over many episodes. There are often many characters in a storyline.

Anime fans sometimes wear costumes of their favorite characters at anime conventions. One popular character is Goku from Dragon Ball Z.

MANY DIFFERENT GENRES

There are many different **genres** of anime. Some anime series are filled with action and adventure. Others tell stories of everyday life. Some of the main genres of anime include shonen, shojo, and seinen.

Shonen anime is known for its action and adventure stories. Shonen often follows young male lead characters on epic quests or adventures. Characters face difficult obstacles. They battle enemies in exciting fight scenes. Shonen often features themes of courage, determination, and friendship. Examples of shonen anime include *Dragon Ball Z* and *Naruto*. These anime series are based on popular Japanese manga comics. There are several subgenres of shonen anime. They include sports, fantasy, science fiction, and horror stories.

Shojo anime focus on romance and drama. This type of anime often stars a young female character. She experiences the highs and lows of love and relationships. As characters face life's challenges, they learn about themselves. Examples of

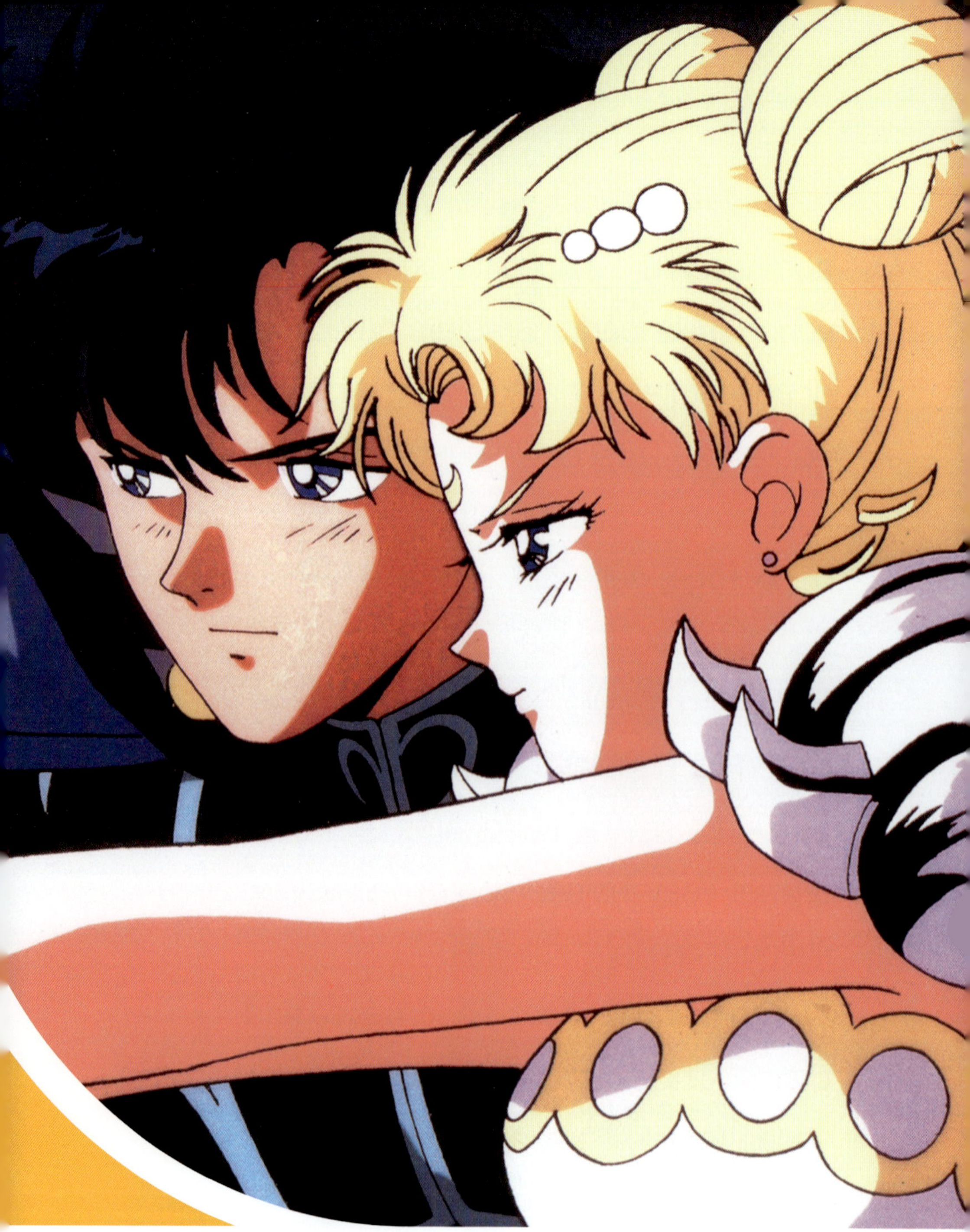

In addition to romance, shojo anime series often feature strong female characters.

shojo anime include *Sailor Moon* and *Fruits Basket*.

Seinen anime appeals to young adults. Seinen means "youth" in Japanese. These shows often include darker, more complex storylines and characters. Seinen may include mature themes such as violence, sex, and politics. Examples of seinen anime include *Death Note* and *Monster*.

LOVED WORLDWIDE

Dragon Ball is one of the most popular anime of all time. The series began in 1986. The show follows the adventures of a young boy named Goku. He searches for seven dragon balls. When combined, these magical spheres can grant their owner one wish. As Goku searches for the balls, he trains to become the world's strongest fighter. The show has many fight scenes. Goku makes new friends and enemies during his adventures. The original series's success led to many spinoffs and sequels over 30 years. They include the long-running *Dragon Ball Z*.

Spencer Dinwiddie is a guard for the Brooklyn Nets basketball team. *Dragon Ball Z* became his favorite show as a child. "Who doesn't want to watch a bunch of

JAPANESE CULTURE

Anime gives fans a glimpse into Japanese culture. People who have never been to Japan can learn about Japanese history and folklore through anime. For example, some series discuss Shinto or Buddhist beliefs and mythology. Others show what Japan was like in centuries past.

NBA player Spencer Dinwiddie says his favorite Dragon Ball Z character is Vegeta. Dinwiddie identifies with Vegeta because of the character's drive to become the best at what he does.

guys flying around while they're fighting," Dinwiddie says. He still enjoys *Dragon Ball* as an adult. "To be able to see something come back to life and people still have the same interest is pretty cool," he says. "I still watch every Sunday, and it's like, 'Wow, after all these years, I still love the show.'"[2]

2

HISTORY OF ANIME

Anime first appeared in Japan in the early 1900s. One of the first anime films was *Namakura Gatana*. This means "dull-edged sword." The 4-minute film was released in 1917. The short comedy tells the story of a skilled Japanese warrior called a samurai. He loses every battle he fights because his sword is so dull.

EARLY YEARS

Early Japanese animators experimented with animation techniques from Europe and the United States. By the 1930s, anime was becoming more popular in Japan. However, anime supplies such as **celluloid**

A major earthquake that struck Japan in 1923 destroyed many of the earliest anime films.

paper were expensive. Japanese studios struggled to compete against advanced European and American animation.

In the 1930s and 1940s, animators made films for the government. These films were released throughout Japan. They were used as entertainment to distract the Japanese people from difficulties caused by World War II (1939–1945). The government funding allowed Japanese artists to make new progress in anime.

POST-WAR ANIME BOOM

After World War II, Japan's first modern anime companies emerged. One award-winning studio named Toei formed an animation division in 1956. In 1958, Toei released *Hakujaden (The Tale of the White*

Monkey D. Luffy from One Piece has become one of the most popular characters in anime.

Serpent). The film was 78 minutes long. It was the first feature-length color anime film. Toei later produced many well-known anime television series. They include *Dragon Ball*, *Sailor Moon*, *Digimon*, and *One Piece*.

Before television, people could watch anime only in a theater or with a film projector. Television brought anime to more people. In January 1963, a new anime television series debuted in Japan. It was called *Tetsuwan Atom (Astro Boy)*. The series was based on a popular manga. It featured a robot boy who lived with humans. He battled criminals, aliens, and other robots. It was the first time an anime series appeared on Japanese television. *Astro Boy* became a massive success in Japan. Later, it was shown worldwide.

GOING GLOBAL

Anime slowly spread throughout the world in the 1960s. In September 1963, *Astro Boy* aired on American television. At first, many American viewers did not like it. They found the Japanese cartoon strange. It was different from the cartoons they were used to watching.

In the 1970s, anime continued to grow in Japan. Japanese animators tried new styles and content. Some popular anime genres emerged. One example was mecha anime, which features giant robots.

The 1980s are known as the golden age of anime. Many of anime's most popular

OSAMU TEZUKA

Osamu Tezuka was one of Japan's greatest manga and anime creators. He created *Astro Boy*. Tezuka produced more than 200,000 pages of **storyboards** and scripts for almost 500 episodes of anime series. Over his 40-year career, Tezuka won several awards. He is known as the godfather of anime.

Mecha anime, which features robots, became popular in the 1980s. Gundam is among the top mecha anime.

titles, such as *Dragon Ball* and *Akira*, were created during this period. Home video technology expanded anime even more. Some anime projects were released straight to video. In the video releases, Japanese animators got even more creative with storylines and animation techniques. Home video also allowed more people outside Japan to watch anime. By the late 1980s, a new group of people called otaku were devoted to anime. Otaku means “geek” or “nerd” in Japanese. Anime fans embraced the nickname. It showed how devoted they were to anime.

TECHNOLOGY BRINGS NEW INTEREST

By the 1990s, anime was a fixture of Japanese culture. Devoted fans watched anime movies and television series. Animators created new genres of anime to appeal to specific fan groups. Adult interest in anime also grew.

Interest in anime has kept growing since the first New York Comic Con convention in 2006. The event now draws about 200,000 people each year.

At the start of the new millennium, technology brought anime to even more people. DVDs could hold entire series of anime. The internet permitted fans worldwide to share anime almost instantly. Fans could talk about their favorite shows in online forums. Long-running series such as *One Piece*, *Naruto*, and *Bleach* were hits in Japan and other countries. Fans watched the shows and went to anime movies. People played anime video games and proudly wore anime merchandise.

AWARD WINNER

In the early 2000s, anime reached the top of the global movie industry. The anime movie *Spirited Away* thrilled audiences worldwide. The film was directed by Hayao Miyazaki. It is a fairy tale about a girl named Chihiro. She becomes trapped in the spirit world. Critics praised the film. At the 2003

Both anime fans and creators admire Hayao Miyazaki. In 2014, he received an honorary Academy Award for his inspiring work in film.

Academy Awards, *Spirited Away* won the prize for Best Animated Feature. It was the first non-English film to win the award.

Rayna Denison is a senior lecturer at the University of East Anglia in England. She says, "This is a film made by a master animator at the height of his powers, and it is one where the quality of the animation really does set it apart from everything else around it. Nobody else was making films that looked like this or that were as inventive as this was at this time."[3]

Today, anime is recognized worldwide as entertainment and art. Studios are always looking for new ways to tell anime stories. Anime has expanded onto the internet and mobile devices. Technology even allows amateur animators to make and upload anime for online audiences. Anime continues to entertain fans of all ages and backgrounds.

3

HOW IS ANIME MADE?

Creating an anime project is a detailed process. At an anime studio, a director leads a team of artists. Each studio has its own style. But almost every project follows the same general process. It starts with an idea and ends with a completed anime. The development process can take months or even years to complete.

START WITH A STORY

Every anime starts as an idea. Ideas can come from anywhere. Some come from

Many successful anime series, such as Naruto and One Piece, were manga before being turned into anime series.

popular manga comics. Other ideas come from novels. And some ideas are original. No matter where it comes from, the story must be turned into a script. Writers create a script with the right length and pacing for each episode. Once the studio is satisfied with the script, the project is approved.

Next, the project enters preproduction. In this phase, the studio plans the project. They get legal rights to use stories from manga or other sources. They also find the artists to work on the project. Some studios use in-house employees. Other times, a studio hires freelance artists to work on a project. These independent artists are not employees. Instead, they get paid by the project. The studio also creates timelines and budgets for the project. Producers find investors to pay for the project.

A storyboard helps the artists plan what the anime will look like as it plays out on the screen.

STORYBOARDS AND DESIGNS

The next step is creating a storyboard from the script. Each sketch in the storyboard shows what will happen in a scene. Storyboards include drawings, camera directions, scene movements, and the length of each shot. The storyboard is a visual guide for animators. It shows them exactly what the director wants to see on the screen.

Artists create layout designs for the background in each scene. First, artists draw these designs on paper. The director reviews and approves the layouts. The layout designs then go to the landscape department. This is where artists draw or

LIMITED ANIMATION

Anime uses a technique called limited animation. Animators reuse drawings in later scenes. By doing this, the animators do not have to redraw an entire scene. They can draw only the new elements. Limited animation makes creating anime faster and less expensive.

paint landscapes and other background scenery. Artists used to paint backgrounds by hand. Today, most are created digitally. Using digital art is usually faster and cheaper for anime studios. It also produces cleaner artwork.

DRAWING FRAMES

Once the layouts are finished, the key animators create high-quality key frames. These are usually the first and last frames of any smooth motion. When a character raises an arm, the key frames would be the first and last frames for the arm motion. In the past, artists drew key frames on sheets of transparent plastic called cels. Today, most studios use computers to create frames digitally.

Computers make it possible for animators to create anime much faster than when it was all done by hand.

Once the key frames are complete, in-between artists start their work. Every second of animation can use twenty-four frames to create smooth motion. Creating this many frames is very expensive. Most anime use fewer frames. The same image is used for two or three frames. This reduces the artists' work. It also creates slightly jerkier movement. In-between artists draw all the frames between the key frames. They make sure each animation ends up with smooth movement. A 30-minute anime episode can have as many as 15,000 pictures.

Next, the completed frames are colored and shaded. Each artist receives the same **palette** of colors so the coloring is uniform throughout the project. The colored frames are placed against the background. In modern anime, animators use computers to add elements such as falling snow or moving clouds. Animators use special effects such as lightning glows, blurs, and more. Finally, each piece is put together, creating the finished video.

Music and sound effects are added to an anime after the animation is finished.

ADDING SOUND

After the animation, there is still much work left. Voice artists bring characters to life. These artists create voice tracks for the project in a sound studio. Also, the audio team adds sound effects and music.

Keiichiro Saito is the director of the anime series *Bocchi the Rock!* He worked closely with the show's audio team. "As we moved forward with making the anime, I would consult them on what sounds you'd hear in real life during a particular scene. If realism would give it more **impact**, we would recreate those real-life sounds as-is. But when the real-life sounds would instead serve as unwanted noise in a dramatic sense, I made the deliberate decision to hold back," says Saito.[4]

HELPING FOREIGN FANS UNDERSTAND

Fans who don't speak Japanese can also enjoy anime. Sometimes, editors will add subtitles to anime that will be sent to foreign countries. While characters speak in Japanese, the words appear near the bottom of the screen in another language.

Other times, editors use dubbing to translate anime. First, a scriptwriter translates the Japanese script into another language. The writer watches the original Japanese anime to ensure the new script matches the characters' mouth movements. A voice actor then records the script in a different language. The new audio replaces the Japanese audio.

Dubbing makes it possible for fans to listen to anime in their own languages. But some fans prefer anime with subtitles added to the screen instead.

4

A GLOBAL PHENOMENON

Today, anime entertains people worldwide. Fans proudly wear T-shirts, hats, and other merchandise that feature their favorite anime characters. Anime fans discuss their favorite shows on social media. Fans post photos and videos about popular shows.

Many celebrities enjoy anime. Michael B. Jordan, Keanu Reeves, and Megan Thee

Stallion have spoken publicly about their love of anime. Reeves was a comic book fan growing up. As an adult, he became

In 2022, Keanu Reeves announced that he was voicing a new anime called BRZRKR. It is based on a comic that Reeves cocreated and cowrote with Matt Kint.

interested in anime on television. He says, "I was watching anime . . . and I didn't even know what it was." While working on the movie *The Matrix*, several people recommended anime shows to Reeves. "They were like, 'You need to watch these.' So it was *Akira*, *Ghost in the Shell*, and that's pretty much the start of it," he says.[5]

ANIME'S APPEAL

Interesting characters drive many anime fans to watch their favorite series. Many characters are confident and determined with a positive attitude. Some characters are interesting because they are unpredictable or have flaws. Anime fan Rachel Lefler says, "I liked the villains in *Sailor Moon* as much as, and sometimes

In the Japanese version of Sailor Moon, words for attacks are usually spoken in English. This makes the words stand out from the other dialogue.

Alternate worlds are common settings in anime. There is even an anime genre called isekai, which focuses on characters who find themselves trapped in a new world.

more than, the heroines. I knew that they were evil and they had to be stopped, but they were often sexy, very smart, and had compelling backstories and interesting personalities."[6]

Anime's diverse storytelling and settings also draw fans to this art form. There is a genre for everyone. Artist GreyRadian says, "The variety of art direction in anime means it can cater to many different audiences across different moods, genres, atmosphere, and stories. . . . I think this is why many people across different cultures enjoy anime."[7] Anime also creates fun alternative worlds. The settings are often as interesting as the characters and stories. Many times, the setting is an important part of the storyline.

Anime affects readers in a variety of ways. The art form means different things to different viewers. Some fans say anime makes them feel more confident. Others say it inspires them. Anime also brings people together. It makes them feel more connected. Anime can even teach readers things about themselves.

A BOOMING INDUSTRY

Anime has become a multibillion-dollar industry. In 2021, the industry hit a record high with sales of about $19.76 billion. This income from sales came from several sources. They included anime on television, streaming services, and video. Sales of merchandise, music, and live entertainment added to the anime industry's revenue.

Anime has become a major export for Japan. Anime series created in Japan are sold in countries worldwide. More than 500 animation studios in Japan work to meet the demand for this entertainment form. More studios have formed outside Japan as the popularity of anime has increased. Today, anime studios exist in Europe, Australia, the United States, and other parts of the world.

ANIME COSPLAY

Some anime fans dress as their favorite characters for fun, with friends, or at events. This practice is called cosplay. Cosplayers wear costumes and wigs and carry props to complete the look. Some cosplayers copy a character's movements and speech. Many pop culture conventions include cosplay events.

Anime inspired by Pokémon video games have become some of the most popular anime titles in the industry.

Interest in anime has grown beyond television shows and films. Video games such as *One Piece Odyssey* and *Dragon Ball FighterZ* are based on popular anime series. Fans have fun playing as their favorite characters. They can also interact with other fans online.

Fan groups bring anime enthusiasts together online and in person. Online groups connect people who have similar anime interests. Anime events and conventions allow fans to meet in person.

ANIME FOR EVERYONE

Japanese artists started anime decades ago. Today, anime entertains fans worldwide. From action-adventure to romance to science fiction, there is an anime series for every type of fan. And anime shows no sign of slowing. In addition to video games and merchandise, there are now live-action movies based on anime such as *Attack on Titan* and *Alita: Battle Angel*.

Many people connect with anime's characters and storylines. Watching anime is a fun and enjoyable way for fans to relax. Anime fan Jan stated, "Anime not only makes me happy but also makes me feel at peace. Whenever I'm going through a difficult time, I watch anime."[8]

Some anime have been made into live-action movies based on their stories. Alita: Battle Angel was released in 2019.

GLOSSARY

animation

the process of creating the illusion of movement with drawings

celluloid

a transparent plastic made in sheets and used for film

exaggerate

to portray something as bigger, better, or worse than it really is

genres

types or styles of movies, books, music, or other media

impact

a strong effect

merchandise

goods that are bought and sold

palette

a specific range of colors to be used in a project

pans

moves a camera horizontally to sweep across a scene

storyboards

rough sketches used for planning that show what will happen in film or television scenes

SOURCE NOTES

INTRODUCTION: DISCOVERING ANIME

1. Quoted in Saleah Blancaflor, "Inside Anime's Rise to the Top of American Pop Culture," *Morning Consult*, October 11, 2022. https://morningconsult.com.

CHAPTER ONE: WHAT IS ANIME?

2. Quoted in Alex Wong, "Dragon Ball Z Is Taking Over the NBA," *Slam Online*, March 26, 2018. www.slamonline.com.

CHAPTER TWO: HISTORY OF ANIME

3. Quoted in Kat Moon, "How Spirited Away Changed Animation Forever," *Time*, July 20, 2021. https://time.com.

CHAPTER THREE: HOW IS ANIME MADE?

4. Quoted in "Bocchi the Rock! Main Staff Interviews—Series Director Keiichiro Saito," *Sakuga Blog*, November 26, 2022. https://blog.sakugabooru.com.

CHAPTER FOUR: A GLOBAL PHENOMENON

5. Quoted in Christian Zilko, "Keanu Reeves Says the Wachowskis Helped Inspire His New Netflix Anime 'BRZRKR,'" *Indiewire*, July 24, 2022. www.indiewire.com.

6. Rachel Lefler, "Why Do People Get So Obsessed with Anime?" *Reel Rundown*, March 28, 2023. https://reelrundown.com.

7. Quoted in "Interview with Curator & Anime Artist GreyRadian," *Makersplace*, August 24, 2022. https://rare.makersplace.com.

8. Quoted in Alisha Shaikh, "Why Is Anime So Popular?" *CanCulture*, May 28, 2022. www.canculturemag.com.

FOR FURTHER RESEARCH

BOOKS

Christine Ha, *Anime and Manga*. San Diego, CA: BrightPoint Press, 2022.

Robert M. Henderson, *Quick Guide to Anime and Manga*. San Diego, CA: ReferencePoint Press, 2022.

Nao Yazawa, *Drawing and Painting Anime & Manga Faces: Step-by-Step Techniques for Creating Authentic Characters & Expressions*. Beverly, MA: Quarry Books, 2021.

INTERNET SOURCES

Lisa Marie Cooper, "Anime from Pen and Ink to CGI," *RightStuf*, n.d. www.rightstufanime.com.

Kat Moon, "20 Best Anime Series to Watch on Netflix Right Now," *Time*, December 26, 2020. https://time.com.

"What Is Anime? Everything You Need to Know," *Nashville Film Institute*, n.d. www.nfi.edu.

WEBSITES

Ghibli Museum

www.ghibli-museum.jp/en

The Ghibli Museum features the work of the Japanese animation studio Studio Ghibli. Its website has information about current exhibits and visiting the museum near Tokyo, Japan.

Japan National Tourism Organization

www.japan.travel/en

The website of the Japan National Tourism Organization includes information about visiting places in Japan, including conventions and museums dedicated to manga and anime.

Toei Animation

www.toei-animation-usa.com

Toei Animation is one of the leading anime studios in the world, creating hit shows such as *Dragon Ball*, *Sailor Moon*, and *One Piece*. Its website has information and news about current and future anime projects.

INDEX

IMAGE CREDITS

Cover: © Barcelona Urban Culture/Alamy
5: © Studio Ghibli/AJ Pics/Alamy
7: © Colleen Michaels/Shutterstock Images
8: © zoranm/iStockphoto
11: © Morumotto/Shutterstock Images
13: © Warm_Tail/Shutterstock Images
15: © Red Line Editorial
16: © Sandro Amato/Shutterstock Images
18: © Toei Animation Company/Photo 12/Alamy
21: © Juan Pablo Rico/Sipa USA/Alamy Live News/Alamy
23: © Joseph Kraus/picture-alliance/dpa/AP Images
25: © enchanted_fairy/Shutterstock Images
28: © Nuntiya/Shutterstock Images
30: © Adam McCullough/Shutterstock Images
32: © Matt Sayles/AP Images
35: © Rizky Rahmat Hidayat/Shutterstock Images
37: © Tutatamafilm/Shutterstock Images
40: © Kaspars Grinvalds/Shutterstock Images
42: © Nejron Photo/Shutterstock Images
45: © Laurent Benhamou/SIPA/AP Images
47: © Lev Radin/Shutterstock Images
49: © Toei Animation Company/Photo 12/Alamy
50: © Grandfailure/iStockphoto
54: © Wachiwit/Shutterstock Images
57: © Sitthipong Pengjan/Shutterstock Images

ABOUT THE AUTHOR

Carla Mooney is a graduate of the University of Pennsylvania with a degree in economics. Today, she writes for young people and is the author of many books for young adults and children. Growing up, Mooney was a big fan of the *Speed Racer* anime television series.